better together*

*This book is best read together, grownup and kid.

 akidsco.com

a
kids
book
about

a kids book about

BEING INCLUSIVE

by **Ashton Mota**
& Rebekah Bruesehoff
in partnership with *The GenderCool Project*

a
kids
book
about

A Kids Book About books are available online: *akidsco.com*

To share your stories, ask questions, or inquire about bulk
purchases (schools, libraries, and nonprofits), please use
the following email address: *hello@akidsco.com*

ISBN: 978-1-951253-89-9

Designed by Rick DeLucco & Duke Stebbins
Edited by Denise Morales Soto

To every kiddo out there who is living
the life they were always meant to live
and to the grownups who believe in them.

To all our GenderCool Champion friends
whose voices helped make this book a reality.
We are changing the world: Alex, Bobby, Chazzie,
Daniel, Eevee, Gia, Hunter, Jonathan, Kai, Landon,
Lia, Max, Morgan, Nicole, Sivan, Stella, and Tru.

Intro

This is a book about the choices we make as human beings to help those around us be seen and feel valued. Being inclusive is one of the most satisfying, healthy, and positive behaviors we can teach ourselves and the kids in our lives. It also helps us see the world around us in the clearest possible way. Inclusion starts with opening ourselves up to people who aren't like us, whether that be differences in gender, race, ethnicity, religion, ability— the list is endless! If we're serious about creating a world where everyone feels welcomed, we need to start with inclusion.

So let's breathe life into this beautiful behavior. Let's talk about real examples of being inclusive. Let's learn from 2 remarkable young people who are here to help through the power of their stories.

Welcome! We're so glad you're here.

—The GenderCool Team

Hi everyone! I'm **Rebekah.**

My pronouns are she/her and I love to laugh!

Rebekah

And my name is **Ashton!**

I use he/him pronouns and I love spending time with my friends and family!

Ashton

Ashton and I met through **The GenderCool Project**, and now we are really great friends!

Rebekah

We want to explore
what being inclusive
means and would love
for you to join us!

What do you think?

If that sounds fun to you,
just turn the page!

Have you ever heard the word **inclusion?**

How about **inclusive?**

Weird words, right?

Maybe you've heard them from a teacher or some other grownup but didn't know what they meant.

Well, **inclusion** is kind of like sharing...

BUT B

It's a choice we make
every day to accept people
and believe they're awesome
for being exactly who they are!

Being inclusive means celebrating everyone in all their uniqueness and making sure nobody feels left out!

Rebekah

Growing up, I didn't really feel included.

I always felt like I didn't fit in or didn't belong. At the time, I wasn't quite sure why until I found the word to describe who I was...that word for me is **transgender.**

Ashton

Even though my friends and family sometimes didn't quite understand the way I felt, they always showed they cared, reminded me they loved me, and wanted the best for me.

That made me super happy!

Ashton

I'm transgender too!

When I was born, everyone thought I was a boy, but I always knew I was a girl.

My family loved and supported me, which allowed me to do the things I love like reading and playing in the woods.

Rebekah

Being transgender isn't a choice.

It's who we are.

But being inclusive? Yeah, that's a choice!

Rebekah

Since our families were able to show us what it was like to be inclusive, it became really easy for us to do the same.

Being inclusive isn't about making all our differences the same.

It's about welcoming everyone as they are.

Look! We'll show you.

Have you ever
gone to class late?

It can be a little
awkward, right?

You're nervous and kind of embarrassed because everyone is already there, and now they're all staring at you, and you feel kind of frozen.

But if you look around and see someone smiling at you—it doesn't seem all that bad anymore.

You feel welcome
and like you aren't
bothering anyone
by being late.

Giving a little wave or just having a smile on your face can be inclusive!

It doesn't even matter if you know them that well!

Just say hi.

Sometimes that's all it takes for someone to feel less alone.

But maybe the person who came into class late didn't only feel excluded because they were late.

I know I've had that same feeling, even when I was right on time.

I felt out of place when I was the only transgender kid in the class. It felt like no one would understand, and I was nervous.

Rebekah

Now that I think about it, me too.

Sometimes at school, I look around and I don't see too many people that look like me or my family. It kind of makes me feel like the star of the show...

but not in a good way.

Ashton

A lot of times, people can feel excluded because of their skin color, or their religion, their gender, the way they dress, if they have a disability, what language they speak— and for so many other reasons.

Even though we're all different from one another, we all want to be part of the group.

We all want to feel included.

Differences don't have to be BIG to make us special.

Little differences are just as important!

I LOVE MAC

Rebekah

AN

I LOVE FREN

The fact that we're different brings us closer together because we always have something new to talk about and share.

If we all loved the same things...

that would be boring!

Hey Rebekah,
didn't you just move?

Ashton

Yeah!

This year, I'm the new kid at school.

Rebekah

Honestly, it was scary to walk into school on the first day because I wasn't sure I would make any friends. I didn't want to be left out either.

But when someone came over and asked me what my name was, I felt better knowing I wasn't alone! It turns out we have the same birthday!

Rebekah

Have you ever
moved, Ashton?

Rebekah

Well, no, but every year at my school we have tons of new kids, and this year I made a really cool friend!

One day at lunch,
I was eating with them
and when they opened up
their lunch box, I noticed
that they brought food
I had never seen before.

Ashton

I was kind of nervous because I didn't want to ask what it was and hurt their feelings, but it looked so good that I had to do it.

They didn't mind at all!

They were actually excited I was interested. They even let me try some, and it was delicious!

Ashton

That's awesome!

Rebekah

You see?

It's about making
a genuine effort to reach
out to someone, learn,
and accept them
for who they are.

Rebekah

Actually, another big part of being inclusive is noticing who isn't there.

Who's being left out?

You have to choose
to see who's left out,
then choose to include
them so they feel like they
are a part of things.

Here's an example:

Imagine you and your friends are all playing tag.

Everyone is running around and laughing, having a great time.

Then you notice someone sitting alone.

You could go over to them and
ask if they wanted to play too.

And now you have a **new friend!**

The truth is...

being inclusive is not always an easy choice,

but it's always the right choice.

Thanks for coming on this journey with me and Ashton. We've learned so much about how to be inclusive, and we hope you have too!

Rebekah

It was really fun!

But do you want to hear something really cool?

The journey isn't over. It keeps going!

Ashton

That's right! Go out there and discover all the **BILLIONS** of ways you can be more inclusive in your life!

Rebekah

So take action!
Choose to be inclusive.

IT TAKES PRACTICE, BUT

YOU CA

Continue your journey
of being more inclusive
every day!

Because when we are inclusive, we help others **THRIVE!**

Outro

It doesn't matter where you live, what you look like, how old you are, or how much money you have—everyone has the power to be inclusive. It starts with caring about helping people feel welcomed, valued, and good about themselves.

Here's where it gets interesting: you have to do more than just care about being inclusive. You actually have to do something. Being inclusive means taking action. There are so many ways to be inclusive—the possibilities are limitless! Thank the person at the grocery store who spends all day stocking the shelves, learn how to say "Hi!" in Spanish, or start a conversation with the quietest person in the room.

It's easy to move through life like a robot, just doing our own thing and not worrying about others. We're all so busy, and the easier path is not the inclusive path, but once you become more inclusive, it's like the best french fry you'll ever eat in your life.

One is just never enough.

—The GenderCool Team

Visit us at akidsco.com to discover more stories.